TREES
OF GREAT BRITAIN & EUROPE

Alan Mitchell

ILLUSTRATIONS BY
David More

EDITED BY
Angela Royston

DRAGON'S WORLD

CHILDREN'S BOOKS

Ecology

Trees are not only beautiful to look at. They clean the air and provide food and shelter for birds, squirrels, insects and many other animals. When you are looking at trees, look for the wildlife that lives on them too.

Planners are well aware of the value of trees in towns and cities and you will find many different kinds growing there. In the countryside, however, woods and hedgerows are still being cut down to make larger fields or to clear land for building houses, shopping centres, offices and even fast-growing forest plantations.

Some of our finest trees are hundreds of years old and many of our hedgerows have existed for over a thousand years. We now realize we need to preserve them at all costs. On page 78, you will find the names of some societies who campaign for the preservation of woodlands and the landscape. By joining them and supporting their efforts, you can help to preserve our native trees and countryside.

Country Code

1 **Never break branches off a living tree** or carve your name in its bark.
2 **Don't climb trees**; you may damage them while you are doing so.
3 **Ask your parents only to light fires in a designated picnic area** in a wood or forest and use the fireplaces provided.
4 **Take your litter home.**
5 **Ask permission** before crossing private property.
6 **Keep to footpaths as much as possible** and do not trample the undergrowth.
7 **Leave fence gates as you found them.**

Dragon's World Ltd
Limpsfield
Surrey RH8 0DY
Great Britain

First published by Dragon's World 1993

© Dragon's World 1993
© Text Dragon's World 1993
© Illustrations David More 1990 & 1993

Edited text and captions by Angela Royston, based on *The Complete Guide to Trees of Britain and Northern Europe* by Alan Mitchell.

Habitat paintings and headbands by Antonia Phillips. Identification and activities illustrations by Richard Coombes.

Editor   Diana Briscoe
Designer   James Lawrence
Design Assistant   Victoria Furbisher
Editorial Director Pippa Rubinstein

British Library
Cataloguing in Publication Data
The catalogue record for this book is available from the British Library.

ISBN 1 85028 219 6

Typeset in Frutiger Light and Novarese Bold by Dragon's World Ltd.
Printed in Italy

Contents

Introduction

There are trees everywhere, not just in woods and the countryside but in town parks and gardens too. In the countryside you are most likely to see native trees, those which grow naturally from their own seed and have grown here since the end of the last Ice Age 17,000 years ago.

You can see native trees in cities too, but they have usually been planted. Many other kinds of trees are planted as well. Most have been brought as seeds from other countries (introduced) and a few are crosses between different kinds of related trees.

The more you know about trees the more interesting they are. This book will help you recognize more than their leaves. In winter look at their bark and buds. In spring watch them flower and then produce seeds and fruits in summer and autumn.

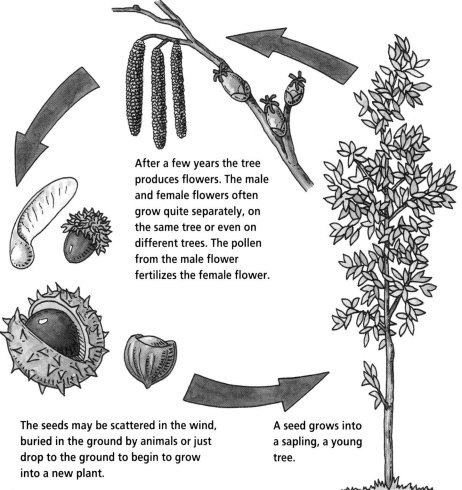

After a few years the tree produces flowers. The male and female flowers often grow quite separately, on the same tree or even on different trees. The pollen from the male flower fertilizes the female flower.

The seeds may be scattered in the wind, buried in the ground by animals or just drop to the ground to begin to grow into a new plant.

A seed grows into a sapling, a young tree.

The Life of a Tree

Some introduced trees become naturalized, that is, they grow naturally from seed like native trees. A few introduced trees have to be grafted on to the stem of a native tree, but most are raised from seeds or cuttings, like the natives.

This mark on the trunk shows where one tree has been grafted or joined on to the stem of another. Grafting is necessary when a tree, like a Japanese Cherry, never produces a seed.

How to use this book

You can use this book to find out more about trees you can already recognize, and to identify a tree you do not know. To identify the two trees shown here, follow these steps.

1 **Decide what kind of tree it is** – broad-leaved, ornamental, evergreen or coniferous. You will find descriptions of them at the start of each section. The tree below has broad, flat leaves so it will be in one of the first three sections. The tree on the left is coniferous, so turn to pages 60–77.

2 **Where is it growing?** If it is growing wild in the countryside it is most likely to be found in the first section. If it has obviously been planted for decoration, start looking in the second section. Only broad-leaved trees that keep their leaves all winter are shown in the evergreen section.

3 **Check what shape the leaves are.** The conifer has single needles, so look through those trees, checking the shape of the tree, the flower and bark against those illustrated. You will find that the tree on the left is a Douglas Fir (see page 64).

4 **If you decide that the tree has been specially planted,** but you cannot find it in the second section, try the first section. Here the trees are arranged according to the shape of their leaves. The tree below has palmate leaves with five lobes. You will find it on page 26 – it is a Norway Maple.

Picture Bands

Each section has a different picture band at the top of the page. These are shown below.

Broad-leaved Trees

Ornamental Trees

Evergreen Trees

Conifers

What to Look For

Parts of a Tree

When identifying a tree, it is important to check more than the shape of the leaves. Look at its general shape and the other parts of the tree shown here.

MALE FLOWERS: most trees rely on the wind to take their pollen to the female flower. Only those with scented blossom rely on insects.
FEMALE FLOWERS: their shape varies from one kind of tree to another. Some are so small they are hard to spot. Others are large and showy.

New BUDS form on the tree in late summer. They contain the leaves and flowers which will grow next spring. Look for the size and shape of buds.

FRUIT: Different kinds of broad-leaved trees produce different kinds of fruit to carry their seeds – berries, nuts, and seeds with wings are most common.

SHOOTS often sprout from the bottom of the trunk. They weaken the tree but make the leaves easy to reach.

BARK is the outside layer of wood. What colour is it – grey like beech, silver like birch or brown like spruce? Is it smooth, like beech, ridged like oak, stringy like redwoods or banded like cherry?

The CROWN consists of the branches, twigs and leaves all taken together. The shape is formed by the main branches and is useful in identifying the tree.

LEAVES make food for the tree from sunlight and water. The size and shape of the leaf will help you identify it.

The NEEDLES on new shoots are brighter green than those on older branches.

Coniferous trees form their seeds in CONES. The size and shape of the cone can help you identify the tree.

The TRUNK is the tree's main stem. It is sometimes called the bole.

Shape of Trees

The overall shape of a tree is a useful clue to its identity. Here are some points to look for:

Many conifers are themselves cone-shaped, narrowing to a point at the top.

Some broad-leaved trees are also tall and narrow.

This tree has a spreading crown.

Do the branches arch downward like a lime – or point upwards like a sycamore?

Many trees have a weeping variety.

Shape of Leaves

When trying to identify a tree, the first thing to look at is the shape of its leaves.

 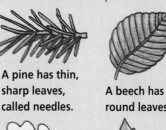   

A pine has thin, sharp leaves, called needles.

A beech has round leaves.

A cherry has toothed, oval leaves.

An oak has lobed leaves.

A sycamore has palmate leaves.

A rowan has compound leaves made up of several leaflets.

Arrangement of Needles

Look at the way the needles of a coniferous tree grow – they are an important clue to identifying it.

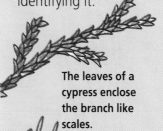 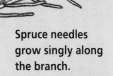

The leaves of a cypress enclose the branch like scales.

Spruce needles grow singly along the branch.

 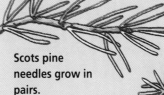

Scots pine needles grow in pairs.

Larch needles form rosettes.

Broad-leaved Deciduous Trees

As you can tell from their name, broad-leaved trees have broad, flat leaves. All the trees in this book are broad-leaved trees except for those in the last section – the conifers. The trees in the first two sections are deciduous, which means that they lose their leaves in autumn and survive the harsh winter weather with bare branches.

Trees in this first section include all the large, common trees that you are likely to see growing in woods or the countryside. Most of them are native trees – that is, they have been growing here for 6–12,000 years and replace themselves with their own seeds. But not all common trees are native. Some, like the Sycamore and Horse Chestnut, were introduced from other countries hundreds of years ago and now seed themselves like native trees. They are known as naturalized trees.

With each common tree are shown several others of similar kinds. Many of these have been introduced from other countries and planted in parks and streets. As you get better at identifying trees you will be able to tell the difference between them and the native or naturalized tree.

Broad-leaved trees grow all over Britain, but some grow better in one kind of soil or climate than another. Although the text tells you where you are most likely to see a particular tree, you may well see it in other areas too. The picture shows seven trees from this book; how many can you recognize?

Ash, Beech, Silver Birch, Blackthorn, Horse Chestnut, Oak, Lombard Poplar

Alders and Birches

Common Alder

Look for alder growing beside ponds, rivers and streams. Notice how its round leaves are notched at the tip, not pointed. They are dark green in summer and are still green when they fall from the tree in autumn. Look for the long male catkins hanging from the tree between late January and April. Look too for the small, red female flowers. These flowers give way to woody cone-like fruits, which stay on the tree for much of the year. They are green at first, but turn brown before opening to drop the seeds into the water to distribute them.

Native
Grows up to 20 m tall
Leaves 4–10 cm long

Italian Alder

The leaves of Italian Alder are heart-shaped and glossy, and the male catkins are longer and bright yellow. The tree itself is more cone-shaped than Common Alder.

Introduced from Corsica and southern Italy in 1820
Grows fast up to 25 m tall

Grey Alder

The leaves of Grey Alder are oval, lobed, pointed and grey on the under-side. They stay on the tree until late November. Notice the smooth, pale grey-green bark.

Introduced from northern Europe
Grows up to 15 m tall
Grows well on dry, difficult soils

You will recognize birches easily by their silvery-white bark and graceful shape.

Paper Birch

You can recognize Paper Birch more easily by its larger leaves than by its bark, which is papery, with patches or tinges of pink, orange or dark purple.

Introduced from North America
Grows up to 25 m tall
Grown here in parks and gardens

Downy Birch

The Downy Birch has a much fuzzier shape than the Silver Birch. Its bark is silvery but does not have the diamond patches that Silver Birch has.

Native
Grows up to 20 m tall
Grows in damp places, alongside streams and in city parks

Silver Birch

Silver Birch grows everywhere, but is most common on dry soils and mountains. Other birches look similar, but you can tell that this is the true Silver Birch by its drooping outer branches and the black diamond shapes on the bark. Birch leaves are triangular and toothed round the edge. The male catkin flowers are easier to spot than the female. Look for the catkins of seed nutlets in autumn and winter. The seeds float down from the trees. Look out too for the birds – redpolls, siskins and tits – which like to feed on them.

Native – Grows up to 25 m tall – Leaves 6 cm long

Beeches

You can tell beech trees by their round leaves with wavy edges. Notice too how smooth the grey bark is.

Copper Beech

Copper Beech is easy to recognize because its leaves are always a deep, red-brown. The shape of the tree and the shape of the leaves, however, are very similar to Common Beech.

Variation
First found in Switzerland
Grows up to 40 m tall

Common Beech

Beech trees grow best on open, well-drained soils. There are many old beech woods growing on the chalky soil of south-east England. They are most spectacular in autumn, when the leaves turn a rich, reddish-brown. The small flowers develop into brown, triangular nuts. In autumn the ground beneath the tree is covered with nuts in their spiny, woody cases. In winter you will still find many of the empty cases on the ground. Look then for the long buds on the bare twigs.

Native
Grows up to 40 m tall – Leaves 8–10 cm long

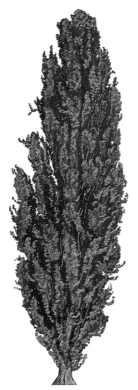

Dawyck Beech

If you find a beech tree with a tall, narrow shape, it is almost certainly a Dawyck Beech. You may occasionally now also see it with deep purple leaves, like a Copper Beech.

Variation
Grows up to 40 m tall
Planted in parks and gardens

Golden Beech

This variation is also called 'Zlatia'. In spring and early summer its leaves are pale golden-yellow, but by August they are just the same as Common Beech.

Variation
Introduced from Yugoslavia
Grows up to 40 m tall
Planted in parks and gardens

Fernleaf Beech

The leaf is deeply lobed and looks more like an oak leaf. The lobes are pointed, however, not rounded. The top of the tree is noticeably lighter green.

Variation
Grows up to 30 m tall
Planted in parks and gardens

Weeping Beech

You can easily recognize this variation from its drooping branches. The tree may be tall and narrow, or shorter and spreading like that shown here.

Variation
Grows up to 30 m tall
Planted in parks and gardens

Limes

You can recognize lime trees from their heart-shaped leaves which are bright lime-green in spring.

Silver Lime

The leaves of this tree are green above and silver below. Look closely to see that the under-side is covered in thick white down. The flowers do not open until the end of July, but then you may find the ground below littered with bees drugged on their nectar. Some Silver Limes have radiating branches, others hang down.

Introduced from Hungary and the Balkans
Grows up to 30 m tall
Planted in gardens and city parks

Common Lime

You are most likely to see this tree planted in city streets, parks and gardens. Greenfly feed on the sap of the leaves, and drop sticky honeydew on to the pavements and cars below. Look for the sweet-scented, yellow flowers that hang below a leafy bract and attract many bees. The flowers give way to clusters of fruit, which drift away from the tree on the long, wing-like bract. Limes grow very tall so those growing in the street have to be cut back, or pollarded, frequently. Look then for the clusters of new shoots sprouting from thicker, older branches. Notice how the side branches arch downwards.

Natural hybrid between Large-leaf and Small-leaf Lime
Grows up to 42 m tall
Leaves 5–10 cm long

Small-leaf Lime

This tree grows wild in woods, but is also planted by roadsides and in gardens. It is similar to the Common Lime although much smaller. Its leaves are smaller too and its yellow flowers, instead of hanging below a leafy bract, shine out like stars in all directions.

Native – Grows up to 32 m tall
Leaves 3–9 cm long

Crimean Lime

This tree is smaller and neater than the Common Lime and does not attract greenfly. It has glossy, dark-green leaves and rich-yellow flowers. It is also known as the Caucasian Lime.

Introduced from the Crimea
Grows up to 20 m tall
Planted in streets and parks

Large-leaf Lime

As its name tells you, the leaves of Large-leaf Lime are bigger than those of other limes. Look too at the side branches. They point upwards instead of arching down. The flowers are the first of any lime tree to open, and the fruit stays on the tree after the leaves have fallen.

Native
Grows up to 40 m tall
Leaves up to 12 cm long

Elms

You can recognize elms from their leaves. They are toothed and oval, with a lop-sided base and pleated look.

Wych Elm

Wych Elms are most common in Scotland and the north of England. Look for them in damp, hillside woods, beside streams on higher ground and in cities. The flowers open first, in early spring, and soon develop into bunches of young, apple-green fruits. Then the leaves open. They are so stiff with hairs they feel like sandpaper. Each seed is surrounded by a broad, oval wing. They turn pale brown and fall from the tree in July to lie thick on the ground. Look too for the Weeping Wych Elm with its hanging branches.

Native
Grows up to 40 m tall
Leaves 15 cm long

Caucasian Zelkova

The leaves are dark green with large, rounded teeth. The trunk is deeply fluted and looks like many pipes stuck together. Look for orange patches on the scaly bark. The tree is often called the Caucasian Elm.

Introduced from Armenia and Azerbaijan
Grows up to 30 m tall
Planted in parks and gardens

The elm-bark beetle, which is only 5mm long, spreads Dutch Elm Disease

Smoothleaf Elm

This tree has also been struck by Dutch Elm Disease and is much less common than it used to be. Its leaves open much later than those of English Elm.

Introduced from Europe
Grows up to 30 m tall – Most common in south-east England

English Elm

This tree used to be very common in southern England until it was nearly wiped out by a fungus called Dutch Elm Disease. The shape of the tree is one way to recognize it. The leaves are about half the size of those of Wych Elm.

Introduced from Europe
Grows up to 30 m tall
Now frequent only in eastern Sussex

Dutch Elm
Disease damage

Southern Nettletree

This tree grows very large in southern Europe where it likes the warmth, but is little more than a bush in England. The leaves have a long, pointed tip and look like nettles.
The fruits are like black berries.

Introduced from southern Europe
Grows up to 25 m tall
Grows only in southern England

Keaki

The leaves are longer and more elegant than those of the Caucasian Zelkova. They turn yellow, pink and amber in autumn.

Introduced from Japan
Grows up to 12 m tall
Planted in parks and gardens

Poplars

Black Poplar

Black Poplar likes the damp soils of river valleys but is being replaced in the countryside by Black Italian Poplar, although you can still see Black Poplar in many cities and by roadsides. The two kinds of tree look similar, but you can tell the native Black Poplar by the large swollen burrs on its rugged grey bark and dense twigs. The four-sided leaves are large and yellowish-green with tiny teeth and a pointed tip. Female and male flowers grow on different trees. Look for the bright-red, male catkins before the leaves open. The female catkins shed 'cotton-wool' seeds in summer on surrounding plants and the ground below.

**Native
Grows up to 35 m tall
Leaves 5–8 cm long**

The leaves of many kinds of poplars are shaped like the symbol for spades in a pack of cards.

Lombardy Poplar

The tall thin shape of this tree makes it one of the easiest to recognize. They are often planted in a line to form a windbreak. True Lombardy Poplars are male trees. Look for the dark-red catkins on the upper branches in early spring.

**Hybrid of the Black Poplar and an American poplar
Introduced from Europe
Grows up to 30 m tall**

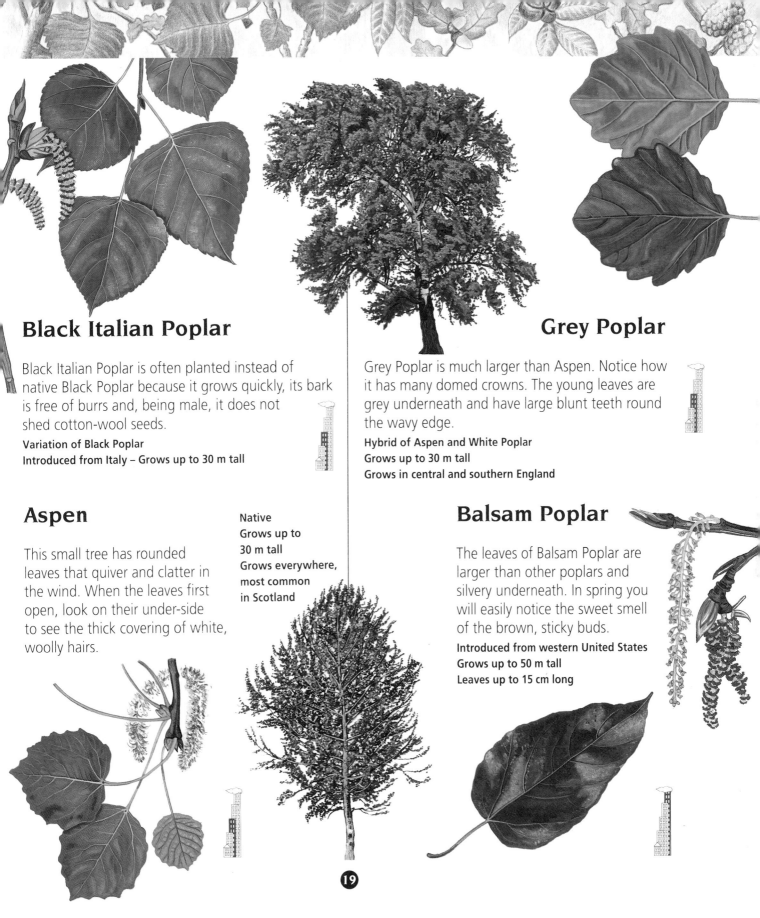

Black Italian Poplar

Black Italian Poplar is often planted instead of native Black Poplar because it grows quickly, its bark is free of burrs and, being male, it does not shed cotton-wool seeds.

Variation of Black Poplar
Introduced from Italy – Grows up to 30 m tall

Grey Poplar

Grey Poplar is much larger than Aspen. Notice how it has many domed crowns. The young leaves are grey underneath and have large blunt teeth round the wavy edge.

Hybrid of Aspen and White Poplar
Grows up to 30 m tall
Grows in central and southern England

Aspen

This small tree has rounded leaves that quiver and clatter in the wind. When the leaves first open, look on their under-side to see the thick covering of white, woolly hairs.

Native
Grows up to 30 m tall
Grows everywhere, most common in Scotland

Balsam Poplar

The leaves of Balsam Poplar are larger than other poplars and silvery underneath. In spring you will easily notice the sweet smell of the brown, sticky buds.

Introduced from western United States
Grows up to 50 m tall
Leaves up to 15 cm long

How a Tree Grows

Trees never stop growing. Every year new shoots grow at the ends of the branches making the crown wider and taller. And every year a new layer of wood forms under the bark making the trunk and branches a little thicker.

Measuring the height

1 **Take 29 equal paces away from the tree**. Ask a friend to hold a stick upright at that point.
2 **Walk another pace away from the tree.** Crouch or lie down so that your eye is as low as the ground.
3 **Look past the stick to the top of the tree.** Ask your friend to raise or lower their hand on the stick until the bottom of their hand lines up with the tree's top.
4 **Measure the distance from their hand to the ground** and multiply it by ten to give you the height of the tree.

Inside the trunk

When a tree has been blown over or chopped down, have a look at the pattern of rings left on the stump. They can tell you the whole history of the tree, because each ring represents the layer of wood formed in one year of the tree's life.

1 **Count the rings to find out how old the tree was.**
2 **Look for rings which are particularly wide or narrow.** Wide rings show years when the tree had plenty of rain and grew well. Narrow rings show years of drought or cold weather when the tree grew only a little.
3 **If the rings are closer together on one side than the other,** try to work out why the tree grew less on the crowded side. Is there a wall or another tree close by?

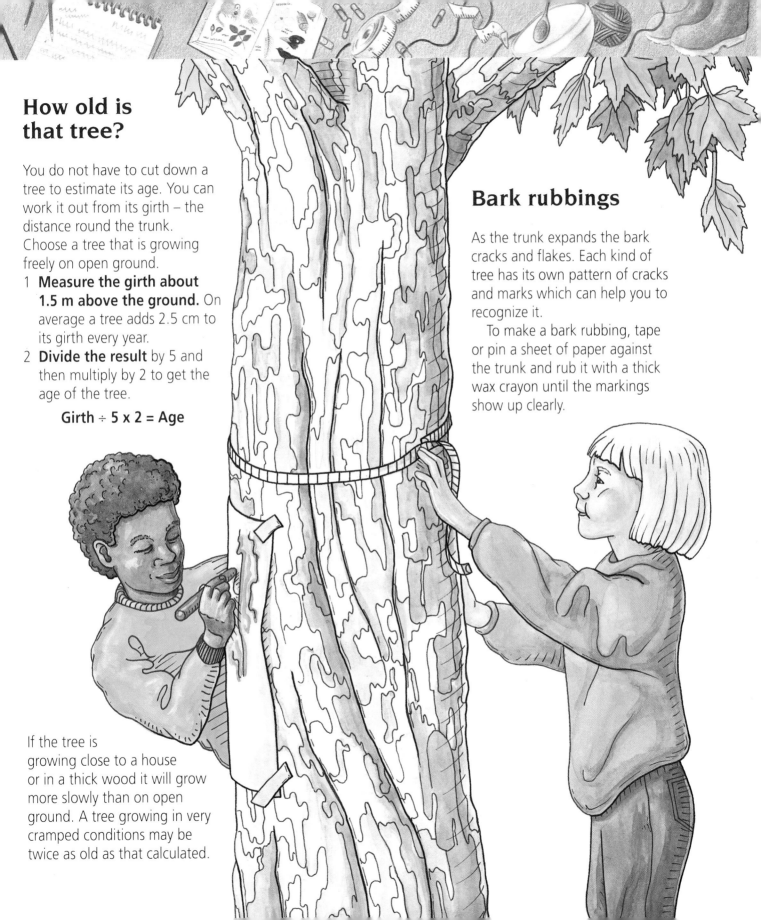

How old is that tree?

You do not have to cut down a tree to estimate its age. You can work it out from its girth – the distance round the trunk. Choose a tree that is growing freely on open ground.

1 **Measure the girth about 1.5 m above the ground.** On average a tree adds 2.5 cm to its girth every year.

2 **Divide the result** by 5 and then multiply by 2 to get the age of the tree.

Girth ÷ 5 x 2 = Age

If the tree is growing close to a house or in a thick wood it will grow more slowly than on open ground. A tree growing in very cramped conditions may be twice as old as that calculated.

Bark rubbings

As the trunk expands the bark cracks and flakes. Each kind of tree has its own pattern of cracks and marks which can help you to recognize it.

To make a bark rubbing, tape or pin a sheet of paper against the trunk and rub it with a thick wax crayon until the markings show up clearly.

Willows and Thorns

Willow trees have long, thin leaves.

Crack Willow

You will find this tree growing alongside streams and rivers. It is called Crack Willow because young shoots break off and float away to put down roots further downstream. It is easy to recognize from its long, glossy green leaves, which often hang in lines from the long shoots. Look out for these shoots in winter and early spring, when they turn deep yellow or pale orange before the leaves open.

Native
Grows up to 18 m tall
Leaves up to 15 cm long

White Willow

White Willow has long, slender leaves which are blue-green above and silvery below. Notice how rough the bark is. One subspecies is called Cricket-bat Willow because its wood is used to make cricket bats.

Native
Grows up to 15 m tall
Grows along streams, but more often planted in parks and gardens

Goat Willow (Sallow)

You are probably most familiar with Goat Willow early in the year. Its silvery-grey buds are known as 'pussy willow'. They turn yellow on male trees and green on female trees. The leaves are oval and leathery. They are dark green above and hairy below. In June look for the white, fluffy seeds, like cotton-wool.

Native
Grows up to 12 m tall
Found in all parts of Britain

Weeping Willow

Weeping Willow is easy to spot from its drooping branches and long slender leaves. Notice how yellow the twigs are, especially in March just as the leaves come out. The catkin flowers are yellow too, and often the male and longer female catkins grow on the same tree.

Hybrid with White Willow
Grows up to 15 m tall
Planted not only by water, good in cities

Thorn trees have sharp spines growing from their twigs and branches.

Blackthorn

You are most likely to see Blackthorn as a shrub in country hedges, although it can grow into a tree. The white flowers stand out against the dark twigs. The blue-black fruits are called sloes.

Native
Grows only 4 m high – Leaves 4 cm long

Midland Thorn

The leaves of Midland Thorn are less lobed than Common Hawthorn, but the two species form many natural hybrids. Split one of the berries to see that Midland Thorn has two seeds in each fruit.

Native
Grows up to 10 m tall
Grows in shady woods with heavy soils

Hawthorn

Hawthorn has lobed leaves like oaks, and sharp spines like other thorn trees. It is most common as a thorny hedge beside a field. You cannot miss it in May, when it is covered with white flowers. If left undisturbed, it will grow into a small, dense tree. Look for it in parks and gardens. In autumn the white flowers give way to dark-red berries. You may see redwings and fieldfares feeding on them and, later, waxwings.

Native
Grows up to 5 m tall
Leaves about 4 cm long

Plumleaf Thorn

The Plumleaf Thorn has broad, glossy, unlobed leaves that turn golden, orange and scarlet in autumn. The fruits fall with the leaves.

Hybrid of Cockspur Thorn,
an American tree
Grows up to 10 m tall
Planted in town parks and by roadsides

Oaks

You can easily recognize oak trees from their wavy, lobed leaves.

Sessile Oak

Sessile Oaks have long leaf stalks, whereas Common Oaks have very short ones. They also form a neater shape than Common Oaks, and so are often preferred for planting in parks and gardens.

Native
Grows up to 45 m tall
Found mainly in
the west of Britain

Common Oak

Oaks grow wild in woods and open countryside, but they are also planted in parks. In May look for the small, dangling male catkins. The female flowers develop into acorns, which provide food for birds, squirrels and other animals. In winter, when the tree is bare, you will still find acorns on the ground below. Oak trees have sturdy trunks and broad, heavy branches. Look for the different kinds of insect galls which grow on them. Notice how thick and deeply ridged the bark is. Oaks live longer than all other native trees, except for the Yew. Many of our oak trees are 200–400 years old. Although their centres have rotted and become hollow, their roots and branches continue to thrive.

Native – Grows up to 50 m tall – Leaves 5–12 cm long

Hungarian Oak

Hungarian Oak grows very quickly. It can reach 30 metres tall in 80 years. There are up to 10 wavy-edged lobes on each leaf. Notice how deep the lobes are. The bark is pale grey.

Introduced from Italy and south-east Europe
Grows up to 35 m tall

Red Oak

The large leaves of Red Oak are more deeply lobed than other oak and have pointed lobes. Look for them in a cold autumn when they turn fiery red before falling.

Introduced from North America
Grows up to 30 m tall

Turkey Oak

Turkey Oak has large leaves, and the acorns are held in a mossy cup. The tree grows very quickly and is often planted in parks and gardens.

Introduced from southern Europe
Leaves up to 18 cm long

Cork Oak

The evergreen leaves of the Cork Oak are not lobed at all, but toothed. The tree does not often grow very tall. Instead its heavy, lower branches rest on the ground. In Spain and Portugal the bark is stripped off every few years to reach the layer of cork below.

Introduced from southern Europe
Grows up to 12 m tall

Cypress Oak

This tree grows straight and narrow and is often planted near buildings. Its leaves are larger than those of the Common Oak.

Introduced from southern Germany
Grows up to 27 m tall

Maples and Planes

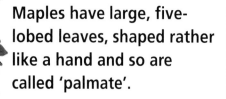

Maples have large, five-lobed leaves, shaped rather like a hand and so are called 'palmate'.

Sycamore

The Sycamore is the largest of the European maples and grows well everywhere, in cities and in country woods. You probably already know its broadly lobed leaves and pairs of winged seeds. Look for the greenish-yellow flowers which appear with the leaves in spring.

Introduced from Europe, now naturalized
Grows up to 35 m tall
Leaves 15 cm long

Field Maple

Field Maple is most common on the chalky soils of southern England. Its leaves are smaller than Norway Maple. In autumn uncut hedges turn dark red and purple, while trees and trimmed hedges turn gold and russet.

Native
Grows up to 20 m tall
Often planted in hedges

Norway Maple

The Norway Maple is smaller than the Sycamore and its leaves are paler green. Notice that the tips of the lobes are much more pointed. They turn butter-yellow in autumn. The flowers are acid-yellow and open before the leaves. Look for early bees collecting their nectar.

Introduced from Europe, now naturalized
Grows up to 30 m tall

Silver Maple

The leaves of Silver Maple are deeply lobed and silvery underneath, giving the tree its name. In North America its sap is made into maple syrup.

Introduced from North America
Grows up to 40 m tall
Planted in parks and gardens

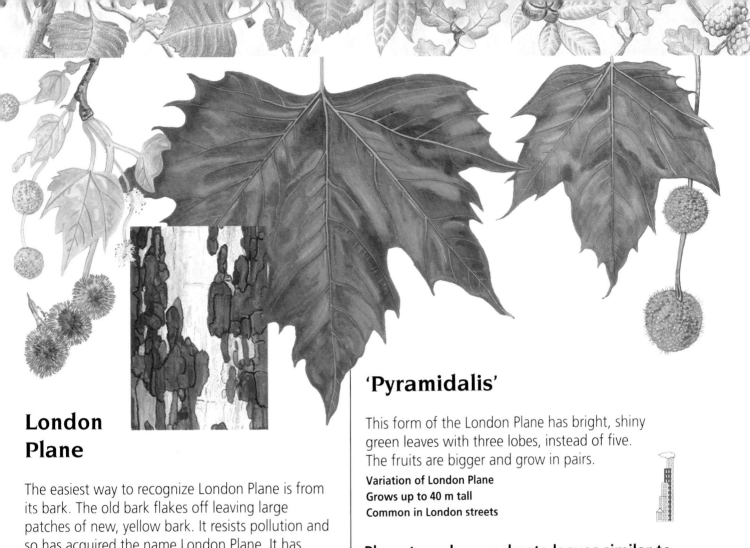

London Plane

The easiest way to recognize London Plane is from its bark. The old bark flakes off leaving large patches of new, yellow bark. It resists pollution and so has acquired the name London Plane. It has rounded flowers followed by spiky fruits, many of which hang on the tree all winter.

Hybrid between Oriental Plane and American Plane
Grows up to 45 m tall
Leaves 15 cm long

'Pyramidalis'

This form of the London Plane has bright, shiny green leaves with three lobes, instead of five. The fruits are bigger and grow in pairs.

Variation of London Plane
Grows up to 40 m tall
Common in London streets

Plane trees have palmate leaves similar to those of maples. To tell them apart, look for the seeds.

Oriental Plane

The leaves of Oriental Plane are more deeply lobed than those of London Plane, and it often has huge, low branches that rest on the ground.

Introduced from south-east Europe
Grows up to 35 m tall
Planted in parks and gardens

Chestnuts

Horse Chestnuts have large, palmate leaves with five to seven leaflets. Sweet Chestnut belongs to a quite different family and has different leaves. It does, however, have similar 'chestnut' fruit.

Horse Chestnut

It is hard to miss this tree, with its large leaves, big, white candle-like flowers and, of course, the shiny brown nuts in their spiky cases. The nuts are used in autumn for the game of conkers. In winter and early spring, look for the large, sticky buds. Look too on the twigs for the horse-shoe shapes which may give the tree its name. They are the scars left by last year's leaves when they were shed in autumn. The 'nails' of the horseshoe show the ends of the veins that went from the tree into the leaf.

Introduced from the Balkan Mountains
Grows up to 32 m tall
Leaflets up to 25 cm long
Planted in parks, gardens and streets

Yellow Buckeye

This tree is usually grafted on to a Horse Chestnut stem. The flowers are yellow or pink. The glossy, bright-green leaflets have short stalks. They turn orange, scarlet and red before falling in autumn.

Introduced from North America
Grows up to 30 m tall
Planted in parks and gardens

Indian Horse Chestnut

You can tell this tree from Horse Chestnut by the narrow leaflets, each of which has a short stalk. The flowers are pinkish. Notice how the dark-brown to black conkers have a thin shell with no prickles.

Introduced from India – Grows up to 25 m tall
Planted in parks and gardens

Red Horse Chestnut

This tree looks very like a Horse Chestnut, but has red flowers instead of white and the fruit does not have prickly spines. It is a hybrid of the Horse Chestnut and an American tree called Red Buckeye.

Hybrid
Grows up to
25 m tall
Common in
parks and
gardens

Sweet Chestnut

Sweet Chestnuts were probably introduced by the Romans, but now grow wild throughout Britain. Look for the very long, narrow leaves. They are toothed round the edge. The long yellow catkins are male, the female flowers may be at the base or on separate shoots. They give way to nuts protected inside a soft, prickly case. Squirrels love the nuts and we cook and eat them too. Sweet Chestnuts can live for hundreds of years. The bark is fairly smooth for the first fifty years, then it develops long spiral ridges. The older the tree, the more twisted is the spiral.

Introduced from
southern Europe
Grows up to 35 m tall
Leaves 15–20 cm long

Ashes

Common Ash

Ash grows well in open woods and along roadsides, particularly on limy soils. The purple flowers do not have any petals. Look for them in spring before the leaves come out. They form bunches of winged seeds, which are green at first, then turn brown. Many of the seeds stay on the tree all winter and are easy to see among the bare branches. Watch out for bullfinches – they like to feed on the seeds.

Native
Grows up to 40 m tall
Leaflets 20–30 cm long

You can recognize ash trees by their leaves, which are divided into many pairs of leaflets with a single leaflet at the tip, and by the seeds with their long wings.

Narrow-leaf Ash

As its name implies, Narrow-leaf Ash has narrow leaflets. They are light and smooth and stand out against the bark, which is rough, knobbly and almost black. Look for the swelling in the trunk about two metres above the ground where the tree has been grafted on to a Common Ash.

Introduced from the Mediterranean
Grows up to 25 m tall
Most common in London, south of the Thames

Manna Ash

Unlike other ashes, the flowers of Manna Ash have petals and a strong scent. They are a bright, shiny green until they open into white showy heads in June. Most of the British trees have been grafted on to Common Ashes. In winter look for the change from ridged Common Ash bark to smooth, dull grey Manna Ash bark.

Introduced from southern Europe
Grows up to 8 m tall
Grows well throughout England and north into Scotland

Caucasian Ash

This is a very beautiful tree with many bright-green, elegant leaves growing on smooth, shiny, pale-grey branches (see above right).

Variation of the Narrow-leaf Ash
Introduced from the eastern Mediterranean
Grows up to 25 m tall
Planted in parks, and recently in streets

Golden Ash

You are most likely to notice this tree in autumn when it is covered with yellow leaves, or in winter when the young shoots are a highly-coloured glossy yellow.

Variation
Grows up to 25 m tall
Sometimes planted in parks and gardens, and on roadsides

Claret Ash

This tree is also known as 'Raywood' Ash. Its leaves are similar to the Caucasian Ash but they turn purple and even dark coppery-brown in autumn (see above left).

Variation of the Narrow-leaf Ash
Grows up to 20 m tall
Introduced from Australia
Planted in parks

Leaves

Leaves are the tree's food factories. While they are making food for the tree, they give off oxygen, which is what we all breathe. So, without plants and trees, all living creatures would die.

Leaves are green because they contain a pigment called **chlorophyll**. This traps the energy of sunlight to make sugar from water from the soil and carbon dioxide, which the tree collects from the air. This sugar dissolves in more water to become sap, the tree's food, which is taken down thin tubes (veins) to the roots where it is stored. During this process, called **photosynthesis**, the tree releases oxygen back into the air. At night, this process is reversed.

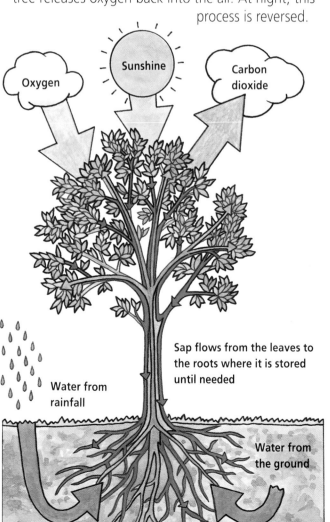

Oxygen

Sunshine

Carbon dioxide

Water from rainfall

Sap flows from the leaves to the roots where it is stored until needed

Water from the ground

Leaf skeletons

You can see the veins in a leaf most clearly when the rest of the leaf has gone. Sycamore leaves are good ones to use.

1 **Boil 1 litre of water in a large pan** and add one tablespoon of washing soda. Ask an adult to help you with this.
2 **Drop the leaves into the pan** and leave them to simmer for half an hour.
3 **When the pan has cooled,** drain and rinse the leaves in cold water and leave to dry.
4 **Use an old toothbrush** to carefully brush away all of the leaf except the veins.

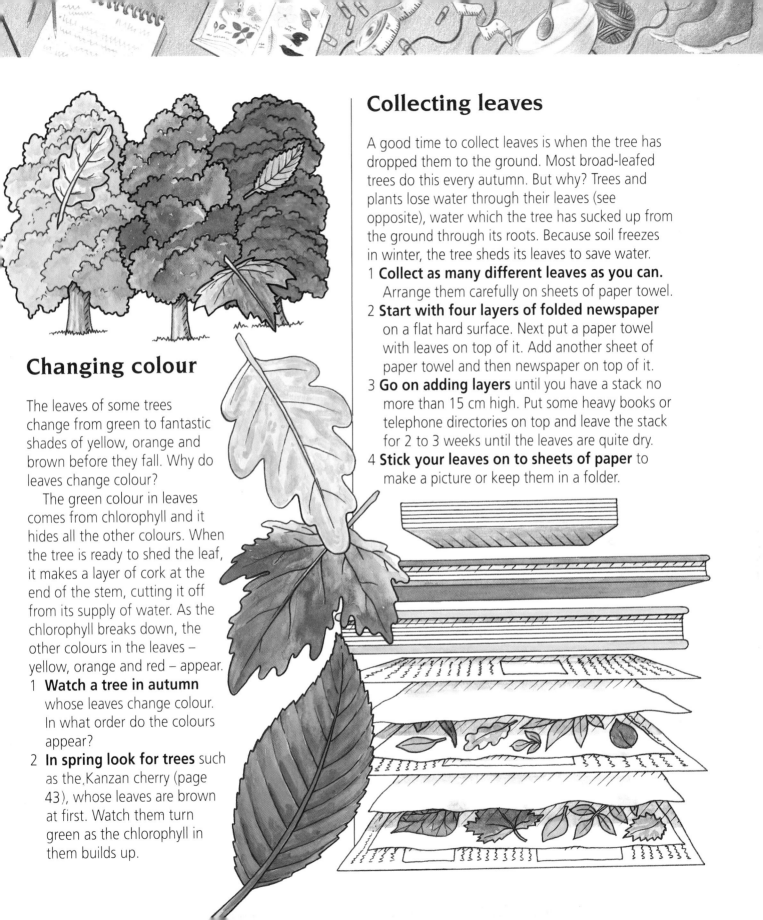

Changing colour

The leaves of some trees change from green to fantastic shades of yellow, orange and brown before they fall. Why do leaves change colour?

The green colour in leaves comes from chlorophyll and it hides all the other colours. When the tree is ready to shed the leaf, it makes a layer of cork at the end of the stem, cutting it off from its supply of water. As the chlorophyll breaks down, the other colours in the leaves – yellow, orange and red – appear.

1 **Watch a tree in autumn** whose leaves change colour. In what order do the colours appear?
2 **In spring look for trees** such as the Kanzan cherry (page 43), whose leaves are brown at first. Watch them turn green as the chlorophyll in them builds up.

Collecting leaves

A good time to collect leaves is when the tree has dropped them to the ground. Most broad-leafed trees do this every autumn. But why? Trees and plants lose water through their leaves (see opposite), water which the tree has sucked up from the ground through its roots. Because soil freezes in winter, the tree sheds its leaves to save water.

1 **Collect as many different leaves as you can.** Arrange them carefully on sheets of paper towel.
2 **Start with four layers of folded newspaper** on a flat hard surface. Next put a paper towel with leaves on top of it. Add another sheet of paper towel and then newspaper on top of it.
3 **Go on adding layers** until you have a stack no more than 15 cm high. Put some heavy books or telephone directories on top and leave the stack for 2 to 3 weeks until the leaves are quite dry.
4 **Stick your leaves on to sheets of paper** to make a picture or keep them in a folder.

Ornamental Trees

Many of the trees planted in streets, parks and gardens have been introduced from countries as far away as Japan, China and the Himalayas of India, as well as from the warmer countries of the Mediterranean. Some are small trees, and you are as likely to see them in suburban gardens as in public parks. All of them are planted because they are particularly decorative in some way.

Magnolias, crab apple trees and, of course, cherry trees are planted for their beautiful flowers and blossom. They are shown in the first ten pages of this section.

Others – the nut, fruit and berry trees – are planted for their fruits. In the countries they come from, trees such as almond and fig are planted commercially for their fruit and nuts, but the British summers are seldom hot enough to make the fruits of those grown here ripe enough to eat. Some kinds of fig tree are evergreen. They have been included in this section because they are grown for their fruit.

Not all the trees in this section have been brought from other countries. Hazel is a native tree that grows wild in many woods and hedges, as are the Rowan and Service-trees, too. They have been included in this section, however, because they are most spectacular in autumn when covered with red berries, and because they are so often planted as ornamental trees. The picture shows nine trees from this book; how many can you recognize?

Almond; Honeylocust; Japanese Crab; Pear; Japanese cherries: 'Kanzan', 'Shimidsu', 'Pissard's Plum'; True Service-tree; Scarlet Oak

Flowering Trees

The trees on these two pages have large, spectacular flowers.

Campbell's Magnolia

You cannot miss Magnolia trees. The huge flowers are spectacular. They open gradually in February and March and can be seen in many gardens, particularly in the south and west of England. The deep-pink flowers of Campbell's Magnolia are followed by glossy, dark-green leaves.

Introduced from the Himalayas
Grows up to 18 m tall
Leaves 12 cm long

Catalpa

Catalpa is also called the Indian Bean-tree. It needs hot summers and flowers best in the south and east of England. The large, heart-shaped leaves do not open until June. The flowers too are very large. Look for the purple flecks on the white heads. The fruits look like long, thin pods, and stay on the tree all winter.

Introduced from North America
Grows up to 15 m tall
Leaves 25 cm long, and wide

Dove Tree

This tree is also known as the Handkerchief-tree because its purplish flowers are surrounded by two large triangular bracts, which look like two large white petals, so the tree looks as if it is hung with handkerchiefs. The fruits are large too – about four centimetres long.

Introduced from China
Grows up to 18 m tall
Leaves 3.5 cm long

Tree of Heaven

The tree grows well in the cities of southern England. The bark is pewter-grey with silvery marks. The leaves, which do not open until June, are deep-red at first, then they change to green. Notice the two large teeth, or small lobes, near the base. They are a good way of telling them from other, similar, leaves.

Introduced from China
Grows up to 26 m tall
Compound leaves up to 50 cm long

Tulip Tree

You can easily recognize a Tulip Tree from its leaves. They each have four points but no tip. They turn gold and pale-yellow in autumn. The flowers are large and look a bit like tulips. They form large brown seed heads, which stay on the tree in winter.

Introduced from North America
Grows up to 40 m tall
Leaves 10–15 cm broad

Caucasian Wingnut

The leaves of Caucasian Wingnut consist of very many pairs of leaflets. The flowers are on a long green catkin and are followed by long clusters of winged seeds. The bark is rugged and twisted.

Introduced from the Caucasus Mountains
Grows up to 35 m tall
Compound leaves up to 60 cm long

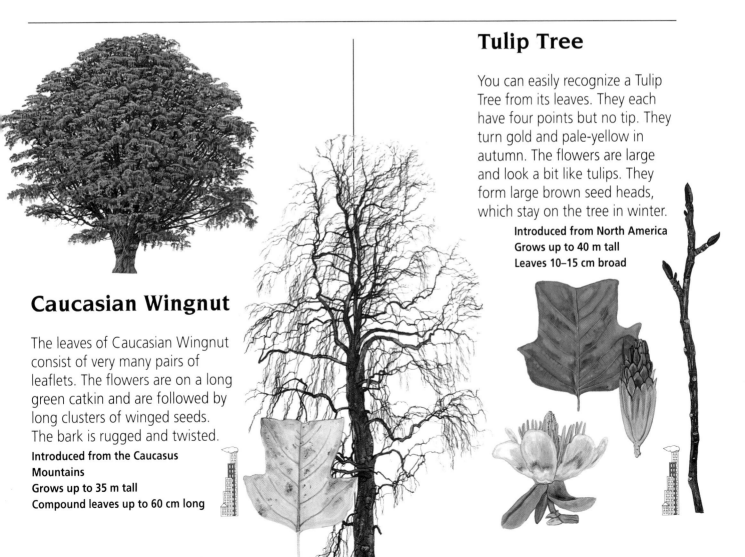

Acacia and Others

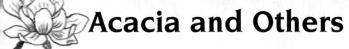

The trees on these two pages have drooping clusters of flowers, or leaves divided into many leaflets, often yellowy green.

Golden Acacia

The leaves of Golden Acacia are the same as those of the Locust Tree except that they are yellowy green. The tree reaches only about half the height of the Locust Tree.

Common in southern England
Grows up to 15 m tall

Pagoda-tree

This tree looks similar to the Locust Tree but has pointed leaflets and no spines on the twigs. Only older trees produce white flowers and pods of seeds. Notice how the branches twist, particularly in the weeping form.

Introduced from China
Grows up to 25 m tall

Locust Tree

Locust Tree is often called Acacia or Robinia. You are most likely to see this tree in gardens in the south of England. Notice how the oblong leaflets stay half folded in cold weather. In warm summers look for long, hanging clusters of scented white flowers. They give way to brown pods of seeds. The twigs have sharp spines and the bark of older trees is deeply ridged.

Introduced from North America
Grows up to 25 m tall
Leaves 15–20 cm long

Honeylocust

Honeylocusts grow best in southern England. Their leaves are divided into many pairs of leaflets. The trunk and branches of the true Honeylocust are covered with groups of sharp spines, but a variety without spines on the trunk is usually planted in towns. The 'Sunburst' Honeylocust is a smaller tree with bright-yellow and green leaves.

Introduced from North America
Up to 25 m tall
Leaves 10–20 cm long

Laburnum

This small garden tree is particularly noticeable in spring, when it is hung with long clusters of yellow flowers. These give way to pods of poisonous black seeds. The leaves are divided into three pointed leaflets.

Hybrid
Introduced from Europe
Grows up to 7 m tall
Leaves 3–7 cm long

Judas Tree

The bright pink flowers of the Judas Tree usually open before the leaves, and grow from the trunk and branches as well as the twigs. They are followed by reddish-purple pods of seeds. Notice how many of the veins on the round leaves start from the base of the leaf.

Introduced from the Mediterranean
Up to 10 m tall – Leaves 7–12 cm long

Crab Apples & Pears

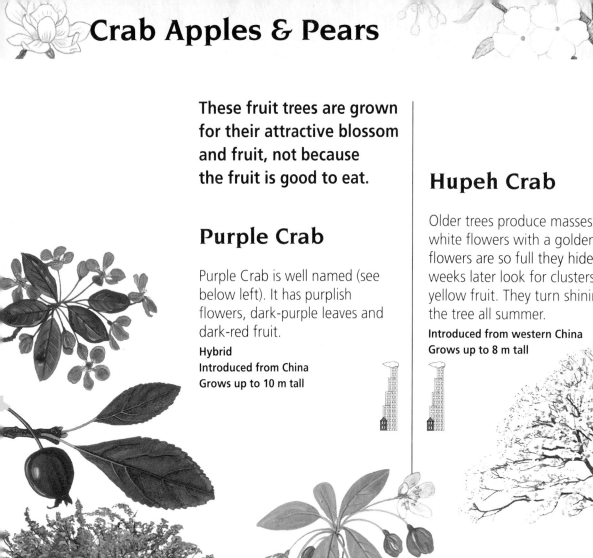

These fruit trees are grown for their attractive blossom and fruit, not because the fruit is good to eat.

Purple Crab

Purple Crab is well named (see below left). It has purplish flowers, dark-purple leaves and dark-red fruit.

Hybrid
Introduced from China
Grows up to 10 m tall

Hupeh Crab

Older trees produce masses of large sprays of pure white flowers with a golden centre. At its best, the flowers are so full they hide the leaves. A few weeks later look for clusters of small orange and yellow fruit. They turn shining dark red and stay on the tree all summer.

Introduced from western China
Grows up to 8 m tall

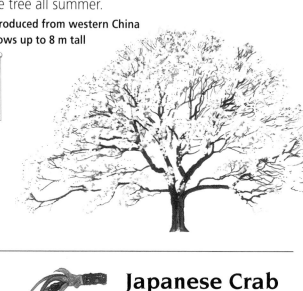

Japanese Crab

This is one of the most popular ornamental garden trees. The oval, toothed leaves appear in March, and by April the tree is covered in pink and white flowers. Every few years it produces tiny, sour, yellow apples with long stalks.

Introduced from Japan
Grows 6–9 m tall
Leaves 4–8 cm long

Chanticleer Pear

This tree is the same shape as the Pillar Apple tree. It is becoming more popular. It often flowers as early as January and the silvery, new leaves unfold before the flowers fade. These soft, grey-green leaves turn yellow, orange and red in autumn.

Upright narrow form of Chinese Pear
Grows up to 12 m tall

Pillar Apple

This neat tree is often planted in streets, precincts and small corners. Its small size makes it ideal for such positions.

Introduced from Japan
Grows up to 12 m tall

Common Pear

You may sometimes see this tree growing on the edge of field, where it is probably the remains of an old orchard. They are often planted in parks and gardens. Notice how the dark-brown or black bark is cracked into small, square plates.

Hybrid of wild pear trees
Introduced from southern Europe, now naturalized
Grows up to 20 m tall – Leaves 5–8 cm long

Cherry Trees

The leaves of cherry trees tend to be longer and slightly narrower than those of apple. The blossom often appears before the leaves. Many cherry trees have horizontal bands on the bark.

Bird Cherry

This small tree grows by mountain streams and in hedgerows. In May the small, white flowers spread in sweet-smelling spikes. They are followed by small, glossy black berries which birds like to eat. The leaves are toothed and are smaller and rounder than those of the Wild Cherry.

Native, but also planted for ornament
Grows up to 17 m tall – Leaves 8 cm long

Wild Cherry

Although this tree is planted for ornament (rarely for the valuable timber), the trees which do produce sweet, edible cherries are varieties of it. Wild Cherry has large white flowers, which appear just before the oval, toothed leaves. The variety 'Double Gean' or 'Plena' has even larger, double flowers. The small, sour fruits are like berries. They become red as they ripen and are eaten by birds.

Native, but planted for ornament
Grows 10–25 m tall
Leaves 8–15 cm long

Sargent Cherry

This tree is very common in towns. The flowers are bright pink and the branches are red-brown. The leaves are sharply toothed and turn scarlet and deep red in autumn.

Grows up to 10 m tall

Winter Cherry

This tree is unusual in that its white flowers open among the yellowing leaves of autumn. The flowers continue to open all winter, become pinker, and double until a final burst of flowers appears in April among the new leaves.

Grows up to 8 m tall

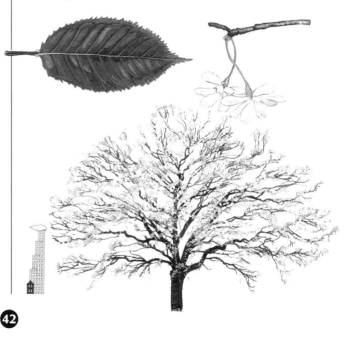

Pissard's Plum

This is a cherry-plum. All these trees have small, single, very early flowers: popular ones have red-brown leaves. The starry white flowers of Pissard's Plum appear first and open from pink buds. The purple leaves follow before the flowers have faded. One variety has rich-pink flowers and shiny, dark-red leaves, and is less attractive to bullfinches.

Introduced from Iran
Grows up to 10 m tall
Leaves 5 cm long

Japanese Cherries

Nearly all the ornamental cherry trees planted in gardens are Japanese cherry trees. There are many varieties with flowers ranging from white to deep pink. Notice the shiny, red bark with its many horizontal stripes. 'Kanzan' and 'Shimidsu' are both hybrids and have been selected from several forms of Hill Cherry. Both have big, toothed leaves which taper to a point.

'Kanzan'

Kanzan is the most popular Japanese cherry and is the first of these to flower. You cannot mistake its florid pink flowers.

Hybrid – Up to 12 m tall
Leaves 10–15 cm long

'Shimidsu'

The flowers of Shimidsu are large and snow-white. They open at the same time as the leaves. The tree has drooping branches.

Hybrid – Grows up to 10 m tall

Nut and Fruit Trees

All the trees on this page, when grown in the right climate, produce edible nuts.

Almond

Almond trees are one of the first to flower in spring. The leaves open after the flowers. They are long and pointed with small teeth. The nuts are enclosed in a pitted shell wrapped in a thin, furry green covering. If unpicked, they turn black and stay on the tree all winter.

Introduced from Asia
Grows 8 m tall
Leaves up to 12 cm long

Common Walnut

You are most likely to see this large, spreading tree beside farm houses in southern and central England, but look for it too in parks and gardens throughout Britain. The scented leaves are divided into rounded leaflets and are bronze when they first open. Look then for the hanging male catkins. The familiar walnut is surrounded by a spongy case, but in Britain they do not ripen enough for us to eat. They are often pickled instead. You can tell Black Walnut from Common Walnut by its bark. Black Walnut has very dark, scaly bark, while Common Walnut has grey, ridged bark.

Introduced from Asia
Grows 23 m tall
Leaves up to 15 cm long

Common Hazel

Hazel grows everywhere in Britain. Look for it in old, managed woods and in hedgerows. It is most noticeable in early spring, when the yellow male catkins hang from the twigs. Look too for the bright-red, female flowers. The leaves are roundish and have double teeth. Squirrels, jays and mice all enjoy the nuts.

Native
Grows 2–6 m tall
Leaves up to 12 cm long

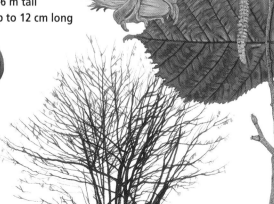

When grown in their natural climates, all these trees produce edible fruits.

Medlar

Medlar often grows as a shrub, and is most likely to be seen in old cathedral and abbey gardens. The leaves are long and crinkly. The flowers are large and white. They give way to large fruits which used to be left on the trees until they were ripe, then stored until they were ready to rot. Only then were they ready to eat.

Introduced from Europe
Grows up to 6 m tall
Leaves up to 15 cm long

Black Mulberry

This tree has been planted in Europe since Greek and Roman times. It is most common in Britain in southern England. It is a short tree with a gnarled trunk and a broad, bushy crown. The large leaves are toothed and heart-shaped. The small, spiky flowers grow into soft, juicy fruits, which are red at first, then ripen to black.

Introduced from Asia
Grows up to 15 m tall
Leaves up to 20 cm long

Quince

In Britain Quince is usually planted in gardens as an ornamental shrub, although in the south it may produce edible fruit. The leaves are oval. Notice how they are smooth on top and woolly beneath. The pink flowers give way to hard fruits. The flowering varieties, Japanese Quinces, have red flowers.

Introduced from Asia
Grows up to 7.5 m tall
Leaves up to 10 cm long

Fig

Fig trees are easy to identify from their large, leathery leaves, which are deeply cut into three to five lobes. In southern Europe they are grown for their juicy, black fruits, which are eaten fresh or dried. In Europe you may often see fig trees growing in walls and steep banks, but in Britain it is usually an ornamental tree.

Introduced from western Asia
Grows up to 10 m tall
Leaves up to 30 cm long

Rowans & Service-trees

All the trees on these two pages produce clusters of red berries.

Hupeh Rowan

Hupeh Rowan has greyish leaves growing from red leaf stalks. The berries are dull white or sometimes rosy pink.
Introduced from China
Grows up to 12 m tall

Scarlet Rowan

In autumn the leaves of Scarlet Rowan turn deep purple, then a flaming scarlet. In summer the fern-like leaves are easy to spot on the downward arching branches. Look too for the long, red buds.
Grows up to 15 m tall
Planted in parks and gardens

Rowan

Rowan grows throughout Britain, and at higher altitudes than any other tree. It is often planted in city streets and gardens. The leaves consist of pairs of oblong leaflets, each up to six centimetres long. The white flowers grow in broad heads and are followed by clusters of berries which turn from green to yellow to red in a few days. From July onwards you can see blackbirds, thrushes and starlings feeding on them.
Native – Grows up to 15 m tall
Leaves up to 25 cm long

True Service-tree

The leaves of the True Service-tree look like those of Rowan. You can tell the trees apart by their bark. The Rowan's bark is smooth, while the Service-tree's is dark brown and finely ridged. The fruits too are much larger.

Native
Grows up to 20 m tall
Leaves 5–9 cm long

Wild Service-tree

Wild Service-tree grows naturally only in old, undisturbed woods, but some are planted for ornament. The leaves look like those of maple and, like maple, turn deep red in autumn. The brown, speckled fruits look more like those of True Service-tree.

Native
Grows up to 25 m tall
Leaves 5–9 cm long

Whitebeam

Whitebeam grows naturally on chalky soil in England and Ireland and is planted in streets and gardens everywhere in Britain except in Scotland. The leaves are silvery-white when they first open, and stay covered with silver hairs beneath. The berries are so popular with birds they seldom last until the leaves turn brown and fall in autumn.

Native
Grows up to 15 m tall
Leaves 5–10 cm long

From Flower to Seed

Some trees have male flowers and others female flowers. The male flowers produce millions of grains of pollen which are blown in the wind or carried by insects to the female flowers on another tree. Some trees have male and female parts within the same flower. When the right kind of pollen lands on the sticky stigma of the female flower it grows a tube down to the ovary where it joins with a female egg to produce a new seed.

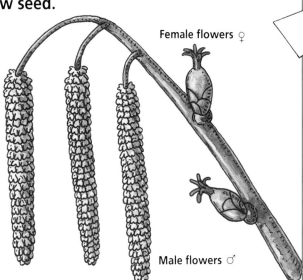

Female flowers ♀

Male flowers ♂

Scattering seeds

Most ripe seeds fall on to the ground beneath the tree, but they have a better chance of growing if they are scattered away from the parent tree.

Many berries are eaten by birds and squirrels who drop the seeds far from the tree. Squirrels and mice bury stores of nuts in the ground to see them through the winter, but some nuts survive to grow into new trees. The wind blows winged seeds on to new ground.

Make a winged seed

1 **Copy this shape** on to a piece of paper.
2 **Cut down the centre line and fold** one wing one way and the other the opposite way.
3 **Pin a paper clip on to the other end.**

Looking for flowers

All trees have flowers. They need them to make seeds. Some flowers are small and hard to spot and some are not coloured or shaped as you might expect. Look out for the different kinds of flowers.

4 **Stand on a chair** and let the shape go. What happens? Does it always twist the same way?

5 **Experiment** with longer and shorter wings, with two or more paper clips, with wider and narrower stems. Which design flies best?

Collecting fruits

Trees hide their seeds inside fruits. There are many different kinds to collect – for example, berries from rowan, cherry and hawthorn; nuts from chestnut, beech, oak, lime, hazel and others; winged seeds from sycamore, maple, silver birch and elm. London planes produce round, spiky fruits while golden acacia, laburnum, honeylocust and catalpa produce pods of seeds. All the conifers produce woody cones of seeds.

Rowan berries

Beech nut

Winged sycamore seed

Horse Chestnut conker

Laburnum pod

Woody pine cone

Bird Cherry has bright, sweet-smelling flowers to attract insects.

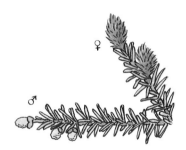

Silver Fir has upright female cone flowers and smaller male cone flowers under the branches.

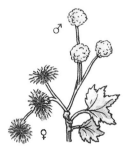

London Plane has round female flowers and clusters of yellow male flowers on the same tree.

Evergreens & Conifers

The first half of this section covers many different kinds of broad-leaved tree, but they keep their leaves on all the year round. However, the leaves of evergreens do not last more than four or five years, and a few are dropping off at any time. If you look on the ground below one, you will usually see some dead leaves there.

Many evergreens have been introduced from hot countries where cold winters are no problem. They survive in Britain only in the milder, damper climate of the West Country.

You can recognize a conifer very quickly by its leaves. Generally, they are thin and sharp, like needles or cling to the branch like scales. The trees in this section have been arranged according to their leaves. Those with scaly leaves are shown first, then those with single, flat needles, followed by those whose needles grow in clusters or rosettes. Then come the pines, whose long thin needles grow in twos, threes or fives. Conifers are most common in cold, northern countries. Most conifers are evergreens, but those on pages 72–73 are deciduous – they lose their leaves in winter.

Conifers belong to a very ancient, primitive group of plants that evolved before the flowering plants. They form their seeds very slowly, often taking months or years. While the seeds develop they are protected inside a cone. The shape and size of the cone are also useful in identifying the tree. The picture shows eight trees from this book; how many can you recognize?

Cedar of Lebanon, Lawson Cypress, Silver Fir, Variegated Holly, Western Hemlock, Monkey Puzzle, Maritime Pine, Yew

Holly Trees

You can easily recognize holly from its thick, shiny, prickly leaves.

Common Holly

Common Holly often grows as a shrub in woods and gardens. When it grows into a tree it makes a cone shape. Notice how the leaves at the top of the tree do not have spines, and are flat compared to the crinkly ones lower down. Male and female flowers grow on different trees so only female trees have the bright-red berries that birds like to eat.

Native
Grows up to
25 m tall
Leaves up to
12 cm long

Yellow-berried Holly

This female holly tree produces yellow berries instead of red. Its dark-green leaves show off the the lemon-yellow berries very clearly.

Native – Grows up to 17 m tall – Leaves 5–8 cm long

Laurel-leaf Holly

This female holly tree has flat, oval leaves without any spines. The berries are red.

Native – Grows up to 20 m tall – Leaves 5–8 cm long

Hedgehog Holly

This holly has rows of spines along the upper side of the leaf, and is often variegated.

Native – Grows up to 15 m tall – Leaves 5–8 cm long

Highclere Hollies

This group of hybrids have flat leaves and are the result of crossing Common Holly with another holly that was brought to England from Madeira in the early 1800s. They are named after the Highclere estate in Hampshire, where the first hybrid was recognized in 1838.

'Hodginsii'

This is the toughest of all the Highclere hybrids and can resist air pollution and the salty winds of sea-fronts. You will see them in cities and seaside towns. The leaves near the base have many straight spines, but those higher up have only one or two spines. The common form is male. It produces purple flowerbuds but no berries.

Hybrid – Grows up to 17 m tall – Leaves 5–8 cm long

'Lawsoniana'

This Highclere Holly is found only as a female tree. Its leaves have no spines and are splashed with varied yellows on dark-green.

Hybrid
Grows up to 15 m tall
Leaves 5–8 cm long

'Golden King'

This is another form of Highclere Holly and has dark-green leaves boldly marked with bright yellow. Some of the leaves are all yellow.

Hybrid – Grows up to 15 m tall – Leaves 5–8 cm long

Camellia-leaf Holly

This Highclere hybrid is a tall narrow tree with bright glossy, almost toothless, long leaves. It bears many red berries.

Hybrid – Grows up to 15 m tall – Leaves 5–8 cm long

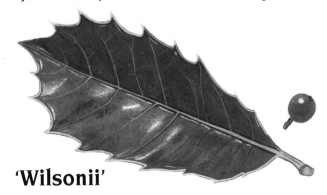

'Wilsonii'

This Highclere hybrid has the most toothed leaves of all this group. The leaves sometimes have a paler edge, as shown.

Hybrid – Grows up to 15 m tall – Leaves 5–8 cm long

Garden Evergreens

Apart from Mimosa, the trees on these two pages have smooth, oval leaves.

Cherry Laurel

The leaves of Cherry Laurel are poisonous, so do not confuse them with those of Bay. You can tell them apart because Cherry Laurel leaves smell of almonds when crushed. Cherry Laurel can take over large areas of countryside. In parks and gardens it is usually trimmed to a bush. Look for song thrushes and blackbirds nesting in it.

Introduced from south-east Europe, now naturalized
Grows up to 16 m tall
Leaves up to 10 cm long

Bay

This evergreen is common in southern Europe and is planted here for its tough, leathery leaves. Crush one to smell its spicy aroma. They are used in cooking to flavour stews. Some bay trees are trimmed to special shapes.

Introduced from the Mediterranean region
Grows up to 20 m tall – Leaves up to 10 cm long

Box

When Box grows as a tree it makes a narrow shape with a pointed top, but you are most likely to see it in one of its many variations that are used for hedges. The small, leathery leaves are glossy green above and paler below. The small, yellow flowers are easy to miss, but look for the woody fruits.

Native
Grows up to 6 m tall
Leaves up to 3 cm long

Portugal Laurel

The long spikes of sweet-smelling flowers open in June. They give way to clusters of black berries. Notice how the leaves grow on red leaf stalks.

Introduced from Spain, Portugal and southern France
Grows up to 15 m tall

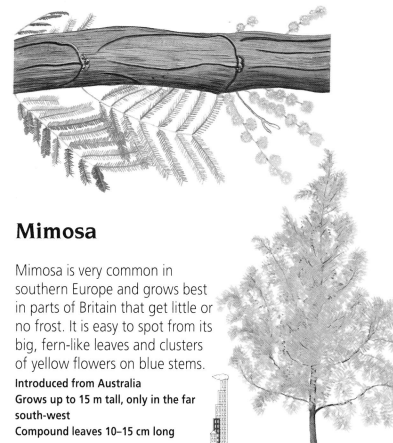

Southern Magnolia

You will see this tree only in southern England, often planted against a wall. Some varieties have brown undersides to their glossy, leathery leaves. The white, sweet-smelling flowers open from midsummer onwards, and may be up to twenty-five centimetres in diameter – as large as a dinner plate.

Introduced from United States
Grows up to 12 m tall
Leaves up to 16 cm long

Mimosa

Mimosa is very common in southern Europe and grows best in parts of Britain that get little or no frost. It is easy to spot from its big, fern-like leaves and clusters of yellow flowers on blue stems.

Introduced from Australia
Grows up to 15 m tall, only in the far south-west
Compound leaves 10–15 cm long

Holm Oak

'Holm' is an old word for holly. When this tree is young its leaves have sharp spines, like holly. Even the adult leaves are not lobed like most other oaks, but are thick and smooth. The fruits, however, are clearly acorns, on spikes.

Introduced from the Mediterranean
Grows up to 28 m tall
Leaves up to 9 cm long

Gum Trees

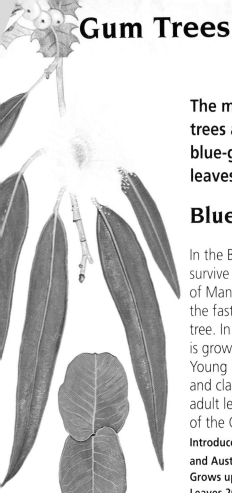

The mature leaves of gum trees are long, slender, and blue-green, but the young leaves are round.

Blue Gum

In the British Isles this tree can survive only in Ireland and the Isle of Man, but in those places it is the fastest-growing and tallest tree. In hot European countries it is grown in large plantations. Young leaves are oval and blue, and clasp the stem in pairs. The adult leaves are longer than those of the Cider Gum.

Introduced from Tasmania and Australia
Grows up to 44 m tall
Leaves 20–25 cm long

Cider Gum

This tree grows well in gardens almost everywhere. The young leaves are blue and almost round. The oval adult leaves taper to a point. Look for the clusters of white flowers from early summer to autumn, although they are produced only by trees over ten years old.

Introduced from Tasmania
Grows up to 30 m tall
Leaves 8–10 cm long

Snow Gum

Snow Gum is the hardiest gum and can be grown in gardens all over Britain. The leaves on some trees are bright orange-brown when they first open. The new red or orange shoots soon become blue-white. Look for the bunches of big, white flowers.

Introduced from Australia
Grows up to 12 m tall

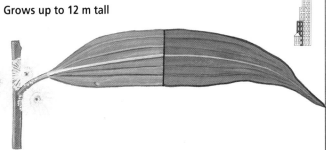

Orangebark Myrtle

This tree grows best in gardens in Ireland and the west coast of Scotland and England. Its orange bark peels leaving patches of fresh, white bark. The leaves are small and oval. Crush them to smell their spicy aroma. Look for the white flowers in August. They are followed by black berries.

Introduced from South America
Grows up to 15 m tall
Leaves 2.5 cm long

Strawberry-tree

Look for this tree on clifftops in southern Ireland or planted in English churchyards and gardens. It grows very slowly, and rarely becomes more than a tall bush. The round, pimply fruit takes more than a year to ripen and remains on the tree with the next autumn's clusters of bell-shaped flowers.

Native to Ireland
Grows up to 11 m tall
Leaves up to 10 cm long

Hybrid Strawberry-tree

This tree grows wild in Greece and is planted in some gardens in Britain. It is a hybrid of the Cyprus Strawberry-tree, which flowers in spring, and the Common Strawberry-tree, which flowers in autumn. It is taller than either of the parent trees and may flower in spring, summer or autumn.

Hybrid
Introduced from Greece
Grows up to 15 m tall

More Trees Needed

Young trees are called saplings. You will see lots of them when you walk through woody countryside, or you can grow your own from pips and seeds.

Choosing a tree for planting

Have you room in your garden for a new tree? Before you rush out to plant a bought one or one of your pot-plant saplings, think about what kind of tree would suit your garden best.

Sycamores, ash and lime grow very large very quickly. You could soon have a monster tree in your garden, blocking out the light and pushing its roots under the walls of the house. Rowan, silver birch and bird cherry are all attractive trees that do not grow too large.

Many garden trees are not grown from seed. They are grafted on to the stems of other trees and can only be bought from a tree nursery or garden centre. They are more expensive than growing your own saplings, but they have been specially produced for gardens.

Grow your own

1 **In autumn collect seeds** from trees such as oak, ash, silver birch and cypress.
2 **Soak the seeds overnight** then peel off their tough outer skin.

3 **Plant several seeds from one tree in a pot of compost.** Cover with more compost and water well.
4 **Leave the pots in a cool place** and wait to see what happens. Don't let the compost dry out.

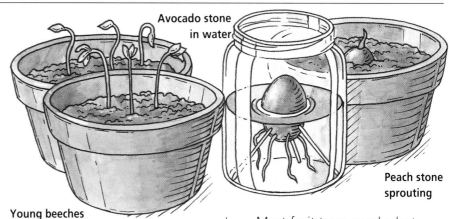

Young beeches

Avocado stone in water

Peach stone sprouting

Exotic trees

The next time you eat some fruit – apple, pear, orange, cherry or peach, for example – save the pips and stones. Soak them in water for a few days, then plant a few of each kind in a small pot of compost. Water the pot well and leave in a cool place.

Avocados have large stones. Soak one in water for a week as shown (above), then plant it in a pot of compost with its tip just showing above the surface.

Most fruit trees need a hot, sunny climate. If any of yours grow, put them in a hot, sunny place, or in a greenhouse. Much of the fruit we eat has few or no pips at all. The trees they came from were grown from grafts and are not very fertile. So, don't be disappointed if many of these seeds do not grow.

Planting your tree

1 **Use a metre of string and two pins** to mark a circle on the ground.

2 **Dig a hole about 50 cm deep.** Loosen any stones or hard earth at the bottom of the hole.

3 **Line the bottom of the hole** with leaf mould or manure to about 15 cm deep.

4 **Push a short stake or post into the hole.** This will support the tree against wind and accidents.

5 **Take the tree out of its container and hold it in place in the centre of the hole.** Spread out the roots and fill in around them with a mixture of soil, compost and sand.

6 **Tread the top soil down firmly and rake it over gently.** Tie the tree to the stake with at least two proper plastic tree ties. Water the tree well and wait for it to grow.

7 **Check from time to time** that the ties are not cutting into the tree. You can remove the stake after about two years.

Ask an adult to help with the digging.

Cypresses

Cypresses all have scaly leaves.

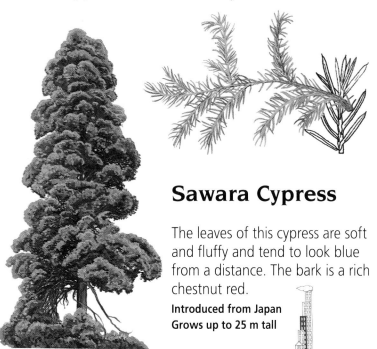

Sawara Cypress

The leaves of this cypress are soft and fluffy and tend to look blue from a distance. The bark is a rich chestnut red.

Introduced from Japan
Grows up to 25 m tall

Golden-barred Thuja

Golden-barred Thujas are often planted in gardens. Instead of the glossy, dark-green leaves of Western Red Cedar, it has lighter-green leaves with bands of gold across them.

Variation of Western Red Cedar
Grows up to 23 m tall

Western Red Cedar

Although the Americans call this tree a 'cedar' it is really a form of cypress. It is planted in large gardens and grows well in the cool, damp west and north. It is also grown for its timber. In damp weather you will easily smell the heavy, fruity scent of the leaves. Look for the scaly cones at the ends of the shoots.

Introduced from North America
Grows up to 40 m tall

Lawson Cypress

This tree can be found in very many gardens. Several varieties have been developed with different shapes, and leaves which vary in colour from dark-green to yellow or blue-grey. The leaves are small and diamond-shaped. Notice how they cover each small twig like scales. Rub them to see how they smell like parsley. Look for the bright-red male cones and bluish-green female cones growing on the same tree.

Introduced from North America
Grows up to 20 m tall
Leaves up to 2 cm long

Nootka Cypress

Nootka Cypress is one of the parents from which Leyland Cypress is formed. It is very hardy but does not grow as fast as Leyland Cypress. Between midsummer and the next April look for the yellow male flowers, and the small dark-blue cones.

Introduced from Alaska and western
North America – Grows up to 35 m tall

Leyland Cypress

This tree grows very tall very quickly. It is often planted in towns and suburbs because it will rapidly form a thick hedge or screen around a garden. The leaves are like those of Lawson Cypress and cover the tree right down to the ground. The tree only rarely forms cones.

Hybrid, developed for gardens
Grows up to 25 m tall

Juniper & Yew Trees

Junipers have a mixture of scaly leaves and needles, and Yew has single, flat, pointed needles. Both Yew and Juniper produce berry-like fruits instead of woody cones.

Common Juniper

You are most likely to see this narrow, cone-shaped tree as a shrub on chalky downs in England, but in pine woods in Scotland it does grow into a small tree. Notice how the needles grow in clusters of three along the stem. The tiny, yellow, male flowers and blue, female flowers grow on different trees. The female flowers develop into dark-blue, berry-like cones.

Native
Grows only 5 m tall
Needles up to 20 mm long

Chinese Juniper

This Juniper is the one you are most likely to see planted in parks and gardens. The young leaves are spiny and hard and needle-like. The older, adult leaves cling to the twigs like scales. Crush them to smell their unpleasant, sour aroma. Notice how the tips of the shoots are paler, even yellow. The fruits are round and blue. Look for the scale marks on them.

Introduced from China
Grows up to 18 m tall
Leaves scale-like outside; needle-like inside, in groups of 3

Golden Chinese Juniper

This tree is most common in towns in southern England. The foliage is bright gold, and for much of the year it is covered with yellow, male flowers, giving the whole tree a yellowish look. These are shed quickly, while the female flowers ripen into cones.

Variation of Chinese Juniper
Grows up to 15 m tall

Meyer's Blue Juniper

This tree is often planted in small gardens. Its needles are electric blue. It grows very quickly for a Juniper.

Introduced from China – Grows up to 15 m tall

Irish Yew

Irish Yews are all females and are as poisonous as Common Yew. Look for them in every churchyard and in large gardens. In western Britain they are often planted in avenues. All Irish Yews descend from one tree found in County Fermanagh, Ireland, in 1770.

Variation of Common Yew
Native to northern Ireland
Grows up to 25 m tall

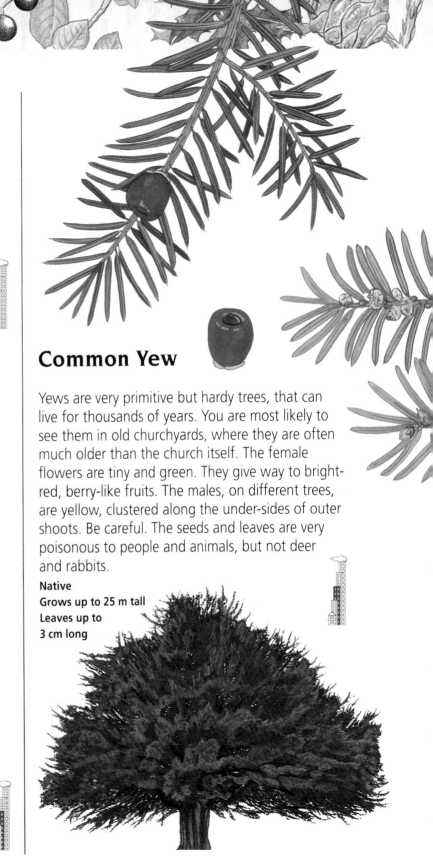

Common Yew

Yews are very primitive but hardy trees, that can live for thousands of years. You are most likely to see them in old churchyards, where they are often much older than the church itself. The female flowers are tiny and green. They give way to bright-red, berry-like fruits. The males, on different trees, are yellow, clustered along the under-sides of outer shoots. Be careful. The seeds and leaves are very poisonous to people and animals, but not deer and rabbits.

Native
Grows up to 25 m tall
Leaves up to
3 cm long

Fir Trees

Fir trees have single, blunt needles. The cones stand upright, except for those of the Douglas Fir.

Grand Fir

This tree grows very quickly and is planted for its timber. The leaves are flat and smell of oranges when crushed. The cones are covered with a sticky resin, and grow near the top of trees, but only those which are more than fifty years old.

Introduced from North America
Grows up to 60 m tall
Leaves about 2–4 cm long

Noble Fir

You can tell this fir from others by the blue-green leaves and the cones with their downward-pointing bracts. As the seeds fall off the cones, only a spike is left. Noble Firs are so tall their tops are often blown out in autumn gales when they are heavy with cones. Look for the thick, twisting branches left at the top.

Introduced from North America
Grows up to 50 m tall
Leaves about 2.5–3.5 cm long

Douglas Fir

This species once had the tallest tree in the world until a 128-metre giant was felled on Vancouver Island in Canada in 1895. The Douglas Fir is not a true fir, despite its name, because it has hanging cones like a spruce.

Introduced from North America
Grows up to 60 m tall

Common Silver Fir

You are most likely to see Common Silver Firs in central Scotland and southern Ireland. Older trees grow very tall. Notice how the older, lower branches fall off, leaving a long trunk of smooth, grey bark. The needles are thick and flat, and paler underneath than on top. The cones are long and slender, but you will see them only if they have been knocked off the tree by the wind or squirrels. As the seeds fall off, a long spike is left behind.

Introduced from Europe
Grows up to 55 m tall
Leaves about 2.5 cm long

Monkey Puzzle

Monkey Puzzles are also called Chile Pines and are easy to recognize from their sharp, flat, thick leaves which cover the stems. Look out too for the round cones covered with pointed scales.

Introduced from South America
Grows up to 30 m tall
Leaves about 4 cm long

Caucasian Fir

The Caucasian Fir is one of the commonest firs planted in gardens. Its branches sweep down to the ground. Notice how thickly covered with needles the branches are.

Introduced from western Asia
Grows up to 50 m tall

Spruces

Spruces have single, sharp needles and hanging cones. The trees themselves are cone-shaped too.

Serbian Spruce

Look for the flat, blunt needles and short branches which give this tree a slender cone shape.

Introduced from Serbia in south-eastern Europe
Grows up to 30 m tall

Norway Spruce

You will know this tree very well because it is the one usually used for Christmas trees. Young trees grow about one metre a year. At one time it was widely planted as a forest tree, but has now been largely replaced by the Sitka Spruce. If you see them growing, look for the long, hanging cigar-shaped cones and the light-brown bark.

Introduced from Europe
Grows up to 40 m tall
Leaves up to 2.5 cm long

Oriental Spruce

Oriental Spruce has thick foliage that reaches down to the ground, and very short needles.

Introduced from Turkey
Grows up to 50 m tall

Sitka Spruce

This tree is the main timber tree of Britain. There are large plantations in Scotland, Wales and Ireland. You can tell it from the Norway Spruce by its scaly, grey bark, spined needles and its small cones with thin, papery scales. The young trees attract plenty of birds, especially finches and warblers, but conservationists dislike large plantations because they leave no room for other kinds of wildlife.

Introduced from North America
Grows up to 60 m tall

The Hemlock-spruces are similar to spruces, but they have tiny cones and soft foliage.

Western Hemlock

Like the Deodar and Lawson Cypresses, the new shoots of Western Hemlock droop downwards. As they mature they straighten and move up. The needles grow in all directions and smell of hemlock, the poisonous plant, although they are not remotely related to it, nor are they poisonous themselves.

Introduced from North America
Grows up to 45 m tall
Leaves 2 cm long

Eastern Hemlock

Eastern Hemlock is a shorter, bushier tree than the Western Hemlock. It has big, low branches and is sometimes planted as a hedge. The leaves and cones are shorter than those of Western Hemlock. With both trees, look for the paler bands of colour on the under-side of the leaves.

Introduced from North America
Grows up to 30 m tall

Redwoods & Cedars

Redwoods and Red Cedars are very tall trees with soft or stringy, reddish-brown bark.

Giant Sequoia

In Britain this tree is probably the biggest in every county. Many in England have been struck by lightning, as you can see from their damaged crowns. In their home in California they are the most massive (though not the tallest) trees in the world, and many are over 3,000 years old. The thick, brown bark is soft and spongy. The leaves are small and slightly scaly. Look for the large, woody cones growing on their own, not in a cluster.

Introduced from North America
Grows to 50 m tall
Leaves 6 mm long

Coast Redwood

Coast Redwoods grow best in the west and north of Britain, but none is as tall as those in California where the largest is 112 metres high. The leaves are flat and pointed. Notice how they are dark green above and almost white below. Look for the yellow male flowers and the lighter green, new shoots at the ends of the twigs.

Introduced from North America
Grows up to 45 m tall
Leaves up to 20 mm long

Japanese Red Cedar

This tree can grow nearly as tall as the redwoods in Britain. It has narrower, scale-like leaves and the cones are smaller and spiky.

Introduced from China, where it is also native
Grows up to 40 m tall

Cedars are large, magnificent trees, with needles that grow singly, or in rosettes.

Cedar of Lebanon

You cannot miss the Cedar of Lebanon with its heavy, spreading branches. Notice how the foliage forms large, flat clumps. Notice too how the needles are bunched together in tufts on the twigs. The tree flowers in autumn and they are followed by barrel-shaped cones which sit upright on the twigs.

Introduced from the eastern Mediterranean
Up to 44 m tall
Needles about 2.5 cm long

Atlas Cedar

Look for this tree in parks and gardens. You are most likely to see the variety which has grey-blue needles. The needles are shorter than those of the Cedar of Lebanon but they still grow in clumps or rosettes. Look too for the upright male flowers.

Introduced from North Africa
Grows up to 40 m tall
Needles 1–2 cm long

Deodar Cedar

Unlike the Cedar of Lebanon, the Deodar Cedar has one main trunk and makes a cone shape. The ends of the branches and the new, young shoots hang down. Its needles are longer than other cedars. Deodar Cedars have been planted in parks and larger gardens everywhere.

Introduced from the Himalayas
Grows up to 50 m tall
Needles up to 4 cm long

Deciduous Conifers

All the trees on these two pages are deciduous – that is, they lose their leaves in winter.

European Larch

This tree has a tall trunk that narrows to a point at the top and sweeping branches. The needles grow in rosettes of thirty to forty on old branches and singly on new twigs. The red flowers are female and the male flowers are golden-yellow. The flowers give way to egg-shaped cones. In autumn the needles turn yellow before dropping. When the branches are bare, look for the graceful sweep of the branches. Notice how they point down, then up again at the tips.

Introduced from the mountains of central Europe
Grows up to 40 m tall
Needles 2–8 cm long

Hybrid Larch

This tree is a cross between the European and Japanese Larches. The cones are longer than on either parent tree. Hybrid Larches grow faster than the parent trees and can perform well in difficult habitats such as thin soil and poor peats.

Hybrid – First raised in Scotland
Grows up to 35 m tall

Japanese Larch

The best way to tell the Japanese Larch from the European is by the orange-red shoots and the shape of the tree. The branches of the Japanese Larch grow at right angles to the trunk, whereas those of the European Larch droop downwards.

Introduced from Japan
Grows up to 40 m tall
Many plantations in central Wales

Maidenhair Tree

Maidenhair Trees are easy to recognize from their fan-shaped leaves and small, soft fruits. The fruits smell awful when they rot, so the male tree is usually planted. Maidenhairs were the first trees – they dominated the forests that dinosaurs roamed 200 million years ago – but they died out everywhere except in China. They were reintroduced into Europe about 1730. Another name for them is the Ginkgo.

Introduced from China
Grows 25–30 m tall
Leaves 3–12 cm long
Grown in parks and gardens; sometimes in streets

Swamp Cypress

The needles of the Swamp Cypress are thin and flat and give the shoots a feathery look. They do not appear on the tree until summer, but they remain until late autumn when they turn reddish-brown. The cones have spiny tips. Swamp Cypresses often grow on flooded ground. Look then for knobbly mounds of wood growing around the foot of the trunk. These take in air for the waterlogged roots.

Introduced from North America
Grows up to 25 m tall
Needles 1–2 cm long

Dawn Redwood

This tree is similar to the Swamp Cypress, except that leaf and shoot grow in pairs, rather than alternately, and the scales of the cones do not have spiny tips. Until 1941 Dawn Redwood was known only as a fossil dating from 80–100 million years ago. Then living trees were discovered in China, and their seeds sent to gardens around the world from 1948 onwards.

Introduced from China
Grows up to 30 m tall – Grown in gardens

Trees and People

We need trees. They are as important to us as to the animals that live in them. Their roots cling to the soil around them and stop it being blown away. They drink in huge quantities of water and slowly release it back into the air. They help to clean the air in towns and cities and, in addition to all that, they add beauty to our lives.

But trees are in danger everywhere, not just in the tropical rain forest. In Britain, too, nearly half of the native trees have been cut down in the last 40 years. Planting trees that will be allowed to grow for hundreds of years is one of the most important things we can do for the future.

Befriend a tree

You can make a record of all the different kinds of trees you recognize or you can concentrate on just one tree, using many of the activities in this book to get to know it really well (see opposite).

You can also help to save trees by recycling paper and buying products that encourage the continued growth of rain forest trees.

Acid Rain

Carbon dioxide is only one of several waste gases that cars, factories and power stations release into the air. Many of these gases are acid and combine with the water in the air to produce acid rain.

Wind and air currents can carry acid rain clouds for hundreds of miles before they fall as rain. You may see acid rain damage in forests in northern Scotland and Scandinavia, far from the cities and factories that produced the poisonous gases.

Acid rain slowly kills the leaves (see page 32). With fewer leaves the tree makes less food and so, slowly, it begins to die. It also harms birds, fish and insects.

Test for air pollution

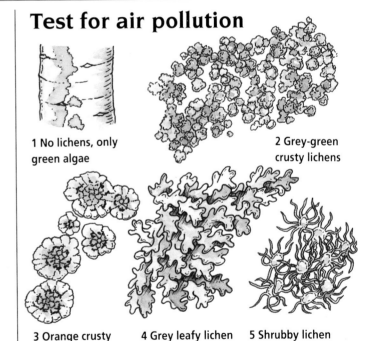

1 No lichens, only green algae

2 Grey-green crusty lichens

3 Orange crusty lichens

4 Grey leafy lichen

5 Shrubby lichen

Lichens are very simple plants which grow on the bark of trees and stones. They are very sensitive to air pollution. Look at the lichens growing in your area and compare them with the pictures above. 1 is from a high pollution area, but 5 is from an area that has hardly any pollution at all.

A tree diary

Choose a tree that you see every day and watch it for a whole year. Write down when it flowers, when new leaves form, when the flowers turn to fruit, and when the new buds appear.

- **Make a rubbing of its bark** and collect some of its leaves to press. Collect some seeds and see if you can grow a new tree from them.
- **Measure its height** at the beginning and end of the year. How much did it grow?
- **Measure its girth** to find out its age.
- **Look for birds, insects and other animals** which use the tree for food or shelter.

12th May – Lime Tree

Green fly were hatching on leaves.

Leaf from lower branches.

Sparrow first seen building nest in top branches at 11-00 am.

Still building at 2-00 pm.

Recycling paper

By recycling paper, you save living trees from being cut down and save energy. Collect cardboard, newspapers and other good quality waste paper from your home and take it regularly be recycled.

Ask your parents and school to buy products made from recycled paper as much as possible.

Pine Trees

Pine trees are easy to recognize from their long needles which usually grow in pairs, although some grow in bundles of threes or fives (see pages 76–77). The best way to tell one pine from another is by the shape of the tree and cone.

Shore Pine

Shore Pines are grown mainly for timber. You are most likely to see them in large forestry plantations on boggy uplands. It has strong, low branches and bunches of short, paired needles. Notice how the trunk often curves at the bottom. The cones are prickly and can remain on the tree for years before they ripen.

Introduced from North America
Grows up to 30 m – Leaves 3–4 cm long

Scots Pine

Scots Pine grows all over Europe, and particularly well in the Scottish Highlands and on the sandy heaths of southern England. Look for the scaly, red bark at the top of the bare, tall trunk and on the branches. Look too for the pairs of bluish-green needles and the small, knobbly cones. The female flowers are pinkish, while the male flowers are yellow and grow only on mature trees.

Native
Grows up to 36 m tall
Needles up to 7 cm long

Austrian Pine

You can recognize Austrian Pine from its black, scaly and rugged bark. In central Europe it is known as the Black Pine. The needles are stiff and sharp and are clustered evenly around the stem in pairs. It is a very tough tree and grows where other conifers cannot. You are most likely to see it in old suburban gardens, on railway embankments, in town parks and near the sea.

Introduced from central Europe – Grows up to 30 m tall
Needles 8–12 cm long

Maritime Pine

Maritime Pines grow well around the coasts of the Mediterranean, and have been planted in large gardens in Britain from Sussex to the Highlands. You can tell it from other pines because the branches form a high, open canopy. The cones are up to twelve centimetres long. When they first ripen they are a shiny red-brown.

Introduced from the Mediterranean area
Grows up to 30 m tall

Mountain Pine

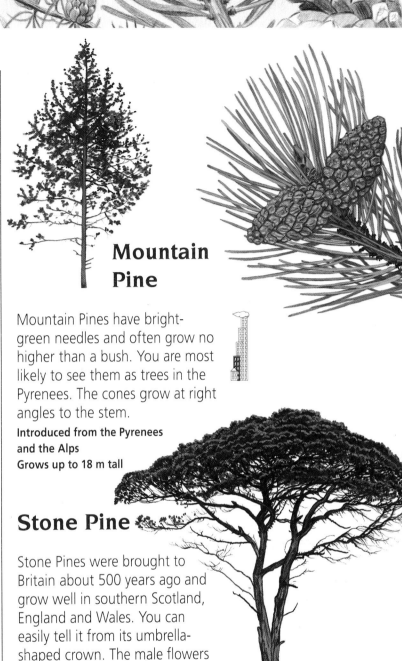

Mountain Pines have bright-green needles and often grow no higher than a bush. You are most likely to see them as trees in the Pyrenees. The cones grow at right angles to the stem.

Introduced from the Pyrenees and the Alps
Grows up to 18 m tall

Stone Pine

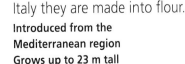

Stone Pines were brought to Britain about 500 years ago and grow well in southern Scotland, England and Wales. You can easily tell it from its umbrella-shaped crown. The male flowers are orange along the base of each shoot. Look out for the woody cones. The seeds are big and are eaten raw or cooked. In Italy they are made into flour.

Introduced from the Mediterranean region
Grows up to 23 m tall
Needles up to 8–15 cm long

Pine Trees

Pines with needles in threes and fives.

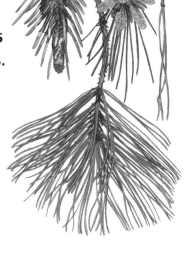

Jeffrey Pine

The Jeffrey Pine forms a beautiful, conical shape with a single, unbranched stem. The needles are greyish and stiff. Notice how dark the bark is. The young cone is purple.

Introduced from North America
Grows up to 35 m tall
Needles in groups of 3,
15–25 cm long

Monterey Pine

This tree grows in many old gardens in the west and south of Britain. The Monterey Pine adapted to surviving California's many forest fires by holding on to its cones until the crown of the tree is burnt. Since such fires almost never happen in Britain, the cones stay on the tree for 20 years or more. Branches can become so weighed down with cones that they snap.

Introduced from California
Grows up to 40 m tall
Needles in groups of 3,
12–15 cm long

Macedonian Pine

Macedonian Pines are tough trees, planted and thriving in many kinds of places from mountainsides to coastal heaths. The dense foliage forms a neat and regular crown. The sticky cones are shorter than those of the Bhutan Pine and so are the needles.

Introduced from Macedonia in south-eastern Europe
Grows up to 18 m tall
Needles in groups of 5, 8–12 cm long

Japanese White Pine

Introduced from Japan
Grows up to 15 m tall
Needles in groups of 5, about 10 cm long

This small tree is often grown in rock-gardens. Its needles are blue-green and the branches are usually heavy with cones. Look for the pinkish male flowers and tiny, red female flowers. The cones are small with big, rounded scales.

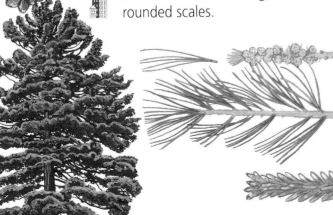

Bhutan Pine

This is the only five-needled pine you are likely to see in or near towns. Look for it in older gardens and parks. The needles are blue-grey, and the bark is pinkish-brown or orange with deep ridges. Feel how sticky the cones are on the tree. The branches point upwards on young trees, become level as the tree matures, and droop in the oldest trees.

Introduced from India
Grows up to 50 m tall
Needles in groups of 5, 10–20 cm long

Montezuma Pine

Although this form is no longer seen in Mexico it is the most common form in Britain. Its long needles are blue-grey, and grow in groups of five on stout, shiny orange-brown shoots. Notice how the tree forms a broad, rather than conical, crown.

Introduced from Mexico
Grows up to 25 m tall
Needles in groups of 5, 30–45 cm long

Find Out Some More

Useful Organizations

The best organization for you to get in touch with is your local County Wildlife Trust. There are forty-seven of these trusts in Great Britain and you should contact them if you want to know about nature reserves and activities in your area. Ask your local library for their address, or contact:

Royal Society for Nature Conservation (or **RSNC**), The Green, Witham Park, Waterside South, Lincoln LN5 7JR (0522–544400).

WATCH is the junior branch of the RSNC and the County Wildlife Trusts. Local WATCH groups run meetings all over the country. Again you can find out about your nearest WATCH group by contacting the RSNC.

The Forestry Commission, Public Information Division, 231 Corstorphine Road, Edinburgh EH12 7AT (031–334 0303). They provide free information sheets about the forests of Great Britain and will tell you how to contact your local branch of the Forestry Commission office, who publish local trail leaflets. There is sometimes a charge for these leaflets.

The Woodland Trust, Autumn Park, Grantham, Lincolnshire NG31 6LL (0476 74297). A charity which owns and manages more than 500 areas of woodland thoughout Great Britain. They also create new woods and replant run-down ones. Their Woodland Rescue programme acts to save woods under threat from felling.

The Tree Council, 35 Belgrave Square, London SW1X 8QB (071–235 8854). They co-ordinate National Tree Week, and recruit adult Tree Wardens to organize tree-planting schemes and tree-awareness activities. Contact them to find out if there is a Tree Warden for your area.

National Trust for Places of Historic Interest or Natural Beauty, 36 Queen Anne's Gate, London SW1H 9AS (071–222 9251). They own more than 570 properties and over 232,000 hectares of countryside throughout England, Wales and Northern Ireland. These include many woods, nature reserves and sites of special scientific interest. Most of this is open to visitors, but you usually have to pay to get into a property. The National Trust also run many courses with school groups; ask your teacher to find out about these.

In Scotland, contact **The National Trust for Scotland** (care of the Education Adviser), 5 Charlotte Square, Edinburgh EH2 4DU (031–226 5922).

Places to Visit

Arboretums are parks and gardens where trees and shrubs have been specially planted. There are many around the United Kingdom; ask your local library or tourist board for details of ones nearby.

Broad-leaved trees: Knole Park, Sevenoaks, Kent; Royal Botanic Gardens, Kew, Surrey; Westonbirt Arboretum, nr Tetbury, Gloucs; Belton Park, Belton, Lincs; Trentham Park, Stoke-on-Trent, Staffs; Granada Arboretum, Jodrell Bank, Cheshire; Castle Howard, N.Yorks; Kilmun Forest Garden, nr Dunoon, Highland; Royal Botanic Garden, Edinburgh; Rowalline, Saintfield, Co. Down, NI.

Ornamental trees: Hillier Arboretum, Ampfield, Hants; University Botanic Gardens, Oxford; Jephson Garden, Leamington Spa, Warks; Dyffryn Gardens, St Nicholas, S.Glamorgan; Calderstones Park, Mossley Hill, Liverpool; Thorpe Perrow, Bedale, N.Yorks; Threave Garden, Castle Douglas, Central.

Conifers: National Pinetum, Bedgebury, nr Goudhurst, Kent; Blackwater Arboretum, nr Lyndhurst, Hants; Lyndford Arboretum, Mundford, Norfolk; Althorp, Northants; Leighton Arboretum, Powys; Skelgill Wood, Ambleside, Cumbria; Dawyck Arboretum, Peebles, Borders; Younger Botanic Garden, Benmore, Dunoon, Highland; Castlewellan, nr Newcastle, Co.Down, NI.

Index and Glossary

To find the name of a tree in this index, search under its main name. So, to look up Field Maple, look under Maple, not under Field.

bract: a modified and often scale-like leaf found at the base of a flower or fruit 15, 64
broad-leaved: trees that have broad, flat leaves 8–62

burr: a roundish growth, like a wart, on a tree's trunk 18

C

canopy: the extent of the branches of a tree 75
catkin: a drooping cluster of flowers 10
conifer: trees that have long, hard leaves (needles) and produce cones for fruit, usually *evergreen* 64–77
crown: the mass of branches and twigs at the top of the tree 7, 19, 77
crinkly: twisted leaves, as in the Holly 52

D

deciduous: a tree that sheds its leaves in the autumn and is leafless for part of the year 8, 70

E

evergreen: a tree which sheds and replaces its leaves gradually all the year round and is never leafless 25, 50, 52–63

F

fungus: a type of plant which grows on other plants 17

G

H

Useful books

The Book of the Forest James Gourier (Moonlight Publishing, 1987).

The Complete Guide to Trees of Britain and Northern Europe Alan Mitchell (Dragon's World, 1985) Large picture book showing more than 600 trees.

The Pocket Guide to Trees of Britain and Northern Europe Alan Mitchell (Dragon's World, 1990) Spiral-bound guide showing more than 280 trees.

The Wild Woods – a regional guide to Britain's ancient woodland Peter Marren (Nature Conservancy Council, 1992).

Woodland Heritage (Nature Conservancy Council, 1990) Describes how woods have been shaped and changed, and also how important they are for our native plants and animals.

Index and Glossary

Endorsed by WATCH

WATCH is the national wildlife and environmental club for young people. It is the junior section of the RSNC, The Wildlife Trusts Partnership, and is the largest voluntary organization in the United Kingdom dedicated to protecting our wildlife and wild places.

WATCH groups throughout the United Kingdom take part in exciting national projects and play an active role in nature conservation. WATCH members receive the club magazine WATCHWORD three times a year. It is packed full with ideas, projects and articles explaining current environmental concerns.

For further information, please send a stamped addressed envelope to the above address.

The Green,
Witham Park,
Waterside South,
Lincoln
LN5 7JR